131968   3.1   ½ pt.

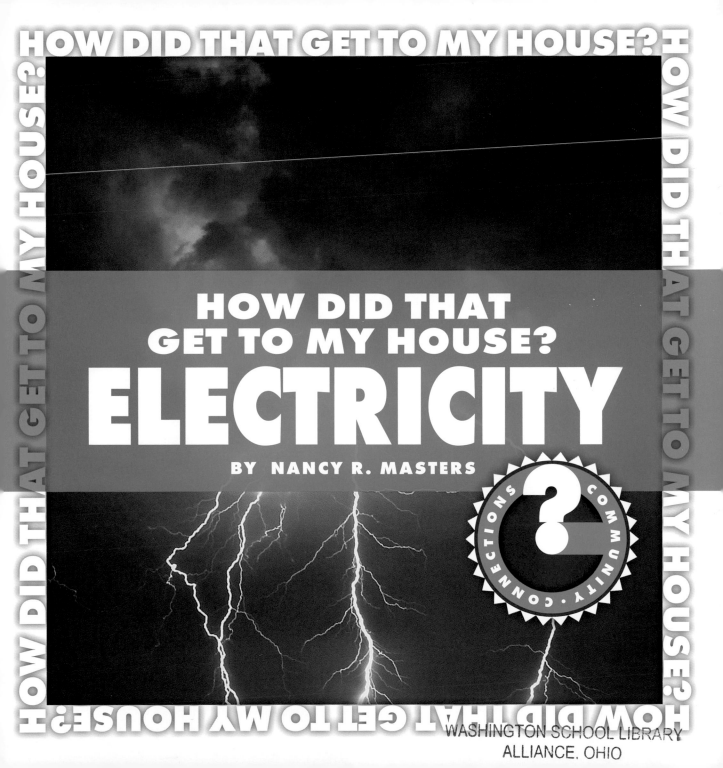

HOW DID THAT GET TO MY HOUSE?
ELECTRICITY

BY NANCY R. MASTERS

COMMUNITY CONNECTIONS

CHERRY LAKE Publishing

Published in the United States of America by Cherry Lake Publishing
Ann Arbor, Michigan
www.cherrylakepublishing.com

Content Adviser: Denise Heikinen, PhD, Sustainable Futures Institute, Michigan Technological University
Reading Adviser: Cecilia Minden-Cupp, PhD, Literacy Consultant

Photo Credits: Cover and page 1, ©Volodymyr Krasyuk, used under license from Shutterstock, Inc.; page 5, ©Eky Chan, used under license from Shutterstock, Inc.; page 7, ©GeoM, used under license from Shutterstock, Inc.; page 9, ©Trebuchet/Dreamstime.com; page 11, ©Chee-Onn Leong, used under license from Shutterstock, Inc.; page 13, ©Freds/Dreamstime.com; page 15, ©Katharina Wittfeld, used under license from Shutterstock, Inc.; page 17, ©Dewitt, used under license from Shutterstock, Inc.; page 19, ©David Gaylor, used under license from Shutterstock, Inc.; page 21, ©Noam Armonn, used under license from Shutterstock, Inc.

LIBRARY OF CONGRESS CATALOGING-IN-PUBLICATION DATA

Masters, Nancy Robinson.
  How did that get to my house? Electricity / by Nancy Robinson Masters.
    p. cm. — (Community connections)
  Includes bibliographical references and index.
  ISBN-13: 978-1-60279-474-0
  ISBN-10: 1-60279-474-X
  1. Electric power systems—Juvenile literature. 2. Electricity—Juvenile literature. I. Title. II. Title: Electricity. III. Series.
  TK148.M37 2010
  621.31—dc22   2008045252

Cherry Lake Publishing would like to acknowledge the work of The Partnership for 21st Century Skills. Please visit *www.21stcenturyskills.org* for more information.

ELECTRICITY

CONTENTS

WHAT IS ELECTRICITY?

You see a light come on. You hear music on the radio. You smell bread in the toaster.

What helps you see, hear, and smell these things? Electricity!

Electricity powers lamps to help you see in your house.

5

Electricity is **energy**. Energy makes things move or change. You cannot see electricity, but it is very powerful.

You need electricity to watch your favorite TV programs.

LOOK!

Look around your house. How many things do you see that use electricity? Which of these could you live without?

7

PRODUCING ELECTRICITY

Houses all over the world use electricity. Where does it come from?

It can't come from lightning. Lightning is too powerful to use in a house. It can't come from batteries. Batteries store electricity. They do not make electricity.

These batteries can't provide all the electricity you need in your house.

Inserite correttamente. Non ricaricare. Respecter les polarités + et –. Ne pas recharger. Auf richtige Polarität achten. Nicht wiederaufladbar. Connect correctly. Do not recharge. MADE IN EC.

9

Most electricity comes from **power plants**. Power plants have machines called **generators**. Inside each generator are rolls of copper wire. The wire spins between special magnet areas. This produces electricity!

The power to spin the wire comes from **natural resources**. These include coal, oil, water, and wind.

Hoover Dam in Arizona is a power plant. The moving water of the Colorado River is used to produce electricity.

MOVING THE ELECTRICITY

The owners of a power plant sell electricity to customers. **Power lines** take the electricity from the power plant to the customers. Power lines are like the halls in your school. They make a path for the electricity to travel. Tall poles hold some power lines high above the ground.

Can you see power lines in your neighborhood?

Power lines take electricity to a **substation**. That is where a machine slows the electricity down. Slowing down the flow of electricity makes it safer. Now it can go into your house.

Many substations are surrounded by fences. Signs warn people to stay out.

Danger
High voltage

Talk to your parents about how to be safe around electricity. Then make a poster that shows some safety rules. Share your poster with other kids. This is one way you can help others.

15

Electricity travels to your house on wires. These wires carry electricity to the outlets and switches in the walls. Outlets connect plugs to electricity. Switches start and stop electricity. Look around the room you are in. How many outlets and switches do you see?

Never play with electrical outlets. Electricity is powerful and you could get hurt.

17

Ask an adult to show you the electric meter at your house. The electric meter counts how much electricity your family uses. Can you see the numbers changing? The numbers change faster when your family uses more electricity.

An electric meter measures how much electricity your family uses.

19

How fast can electricity get from the power plant to inside your house? It just takes a flip of the switch!

Do you need electricity to play some of your favorite games?

THINK!

Think about all the ways your family uses electricity. Are there ways that you can save electricity? Would it be hard to do?

21

GLOSSARY

energy (EN-ur-jee) power to make things move or change

generators (JEN-uh-ray-turz) machines in power plants that make electricity

natural resources (NACH-ur-uhl REE-sor-sez) things in nature that humans can use

power lines (POU-ur LINES) wires that carry electricity to customers

power plants (POU-ur PLANTS) places where electricity is made

substation (SUHB-stay-shuhn) a place between the power plant and your house

FIND OUT MORE

BOOKS

Royston, Angela. *Using Electricity*. Chicago: Heinemann Library, 2008.

Schuh, Mari. *Electricity*. Minneapolis: Bellwether Media, 2008.

WEB SITES

Energy Kid's Page—Electricity
www.eia.doe.gov/kids/energyfacts/sources/electricity.html
Read more about electricity, how it is generated, and how it is measured

Frankenstein's Lightning Laboratory
www.miamisci.org/af/sln/frankenstein/safety.html
Learn about electricity and electrical safety

INDEX

ABOUT THE AUTHOR

Nancy Robinson Masters once lived in a house without electricity. She is glad she now lives in a house that has it. Electricity helps her read and write books.